Cat Chat

by Meredith Phillips

Content Adviser: Professor Peter Bower, Barnard College, Columbia University, New York, New York
Reading Adviser: Frances J. Bonacci, Reading Specialist, Cambridge, Massachusetts

COMPASS POINT BOOKS

MINNEAPOLIS, MINNESOTA

Compass Point Books
3109 West 50th Street, #115
Minneapolis, MN 55410

Visit Compass Point Books on the Internet at *www.compasspointbooks.com*
or e-mail your request to *custserv@compasspointbooks.com*

Photographs ©: Arthur Tilley/Getty Images, cover; PhotoDisc, 3; Christie's Images/SuperStock, 4; PhotoSpin, 5;PhotoDisc, 6; Corel, 7 (bottom center); Photos.com, 7 (top right), 7 (bottom right); Royalty-Free/Corbis, 10; Photos.com, 11; PhotoDisc, 12 (top right); Corel, 12 (center right),12 (bottom right),13 (center top left), 13 (bottom); Photos.com, 13 (top left),13 (center); PhotoDisc, 13 (center bottom left); Photos.com, 15; PhotoDisc, 16; Photos.com, 17; Bonnie Kamin/Index Stock,18; PhotoSpin, 19; Royalty-Free/Corbis, 21; PhotoSpin, 22; Bill Smith Studio, 23 (top); PhotoSpin, 23 (bottom), 24; Photos.com, 25; Corel, 26 (bottom right); PhotoDisc, 26 (center left); Clipart.com, 26 (top right), 27 (top left),27 (bottom left), 27 (top right); PhotoDisc, 27 (bottom right); Clipart.com, 28 (bottom left), 28 (top center); PhotoDisc, 28 (top center right); Comstock, 29 (center left); Alinari Archives/Corbis, 29 (bottom center); Corbis, 29 (top right); Corel, 29 (bottom right); PhotoDisc, 31.

Creative Director: Terri Foley
Managing Editor: Catherine Neitge
Editors: Sandra E. Will/Bill SMITH STUDIO and Jennifer VanVoorst
Photo Researchers: Christie Silver and Tanya Guerrero/Bill SMITH STUDIO
Designers: Brock Waldron, Ron Leighton, and Brian Kobberger/Bill SMITH STUDIO and Les Tranby
Educational Consultant: Diane Smolinski

Library of Congress Cataloging-in-Publication Data
    Phillips, Meredith, 1971–
    Cat chat / by Meredith Phillips.
    p. cm. — (Pet's point of view)
    Includes index.
    ISBN 0-7565-0697-2 (hardcover)
    1. Cats—Juvenile literature. 2. Cats—Miscellanea—Juvenile literature. I. Title. II. Series.
    SF445.7.P48 2005
    636.8—dc22   2004001981

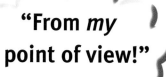
"From *my* point of view!"

Table of Contents

NOTE: In this book, words that are defined in Words to Know are in **bold** the first time they appear in the text.

Who Is Your Cat?

You and Your Cat

Animal Almanac

Wildcats to House Cats

When you look at a cat like me, what do you think? Mysterious? Independent? Agile? That is what the ancient Egyptians probably saw when they brought my wild ancestors into their villages more than 4,000 years ago.

House cats like me come from a line of African bobtailed wildcats. Farmers near the Nile River liked having these wildcats around. They protected the Egyptians' food from rats and mice and were also good defenders against deadly snakes.

The Egyptians fed the cats, and the cats became dependent on the easy source of food. Surprisingly, they also enjoyed the affection they received from humans. As people bred them over time, these ancient wildcats became us—the snuggly **felines** you now love.

The ancient Egyptians often showed their love and respect for cats through art. The Egyptians also depicted many of their gods in cat statues. The famous Sphinx (at right) once had cat paws.

It's All Relative

All **domestic** cats like me are related to wild cats, such as lions, tigers, jaguars, and cheetahs. In fact, the skeletal structures, highly adapted eyes, and hunting prowess are recognizably similar in all of us. You can tell that house cats and wild cats are all close relatives by the way we move, use our claws, and attack.

Among the millions of domestic cats in the world, only about 50 types are **pedigreed** and have papers proving their lineage, or line of ancestry. These are the types of cats most likely to be judged in cat shows. Most of us, however, come from animal shelters or friends and neighbors.

Whatever our background, cats come in all shapes, sizes, colors, and patterns: long-haired, short-haired, slim, sleek, striped, petite, stubby, with folded ears, and with no tails. Some of us even have curly fur! From orange-striped tabbies to colorful calicoes, each of us is unique.

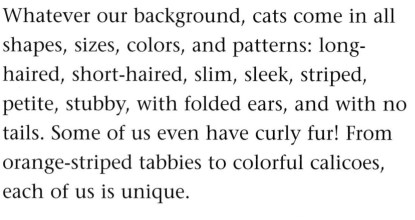
Domestic calico cat

The skeletons of house cats are similar to the skeletons of larger cats, such as panthers or tigers.

Young wild puma

The Way I Work

Even the most pampered house cat like me is not far from being a wild predator. From my incredible climbing abilities to my balance and sense of where I am, my body is designed to help me survive and thrive in the wild.

My claws are one of my special features. They come out and retract depending on how I feel and what I am doing. The razor sharpness and curved angle of these claws make it easy for me to climb things. I keep them sharp by scratching. Outside, I scratch on a tree, but inside, watch out for the furniture! Some owners remove cats' front claws, but we are defenseless without them. Many people think it is cruel to have them removed. If you do remove my claws, though, make sure I always stay inside where I am safe.

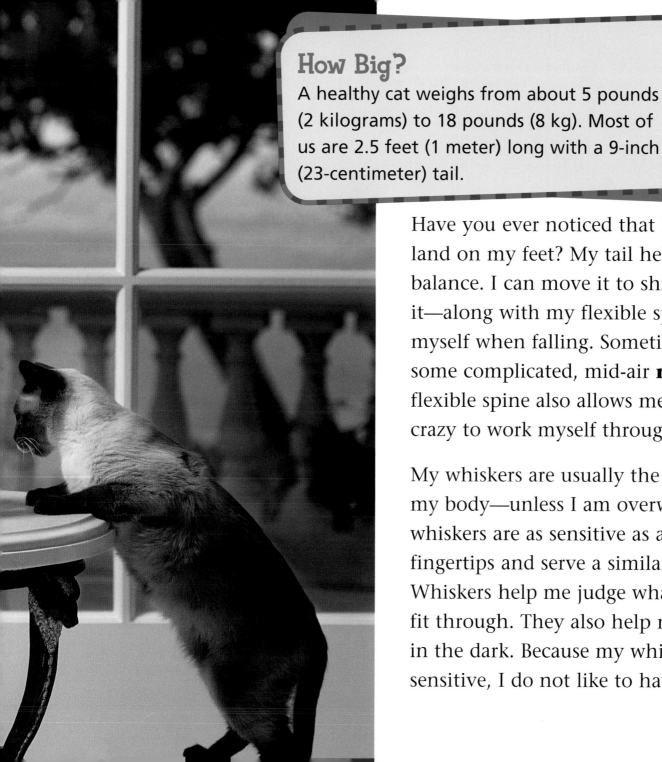

How Big?

A healthy cat weighs from about 5 pounds (2 kilograms) to 18 pounds (8 kg). Most of us are 2.5 feet (1 meter) long with a 9-inch (23-centimeter) tail.

Have you ever noticed that I almost always land on my feet? My tail helps me keep my balance. I can move it to shift weight, or use it—along with my flexible spine—to right myself when falling. Sometimes this involves some complicated, mid-air **maneuvers.** My flexible spine also allows me to wriggle like crazy to work myself through a small space.

My whiskers are usually the same width as my body—unless I am overweight. These whiskers are as sensitive as a human's fingertips and serve a similar purpose. Whiskers help me judge what spaces I can fit through. They also help me feel my way in the dark. Because my whiskers are so sensitive, I do not like to have them touched.

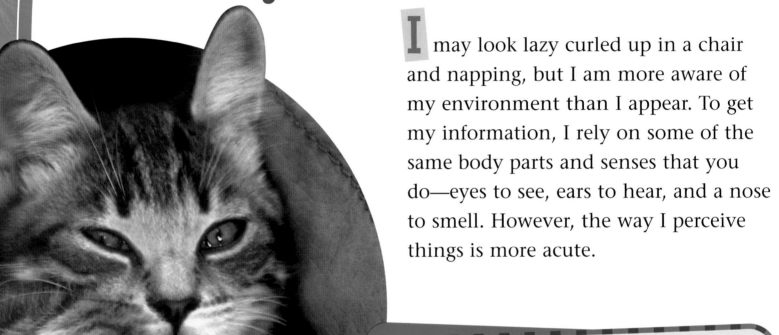

Super Senses

A Cat's Eye View

I may look lazy curled up in a chair and napping, but I am more aware of my environment than I appear. To get my information, I rely on some of the same body parts and senses that you do—eyes to see, ears to hear, and a nose to smell. However, the way I perceive things is more acute.

Sniffing It Out

I can "read" smells to find out about my environment. When my owners arrive home, I will often sniff the soles of their shoes or the cuffs of their pants to see what is going on in the outside world.

Ears: I can rotate my ears 180 degrees to focus on a particular sound, and I have a greater range of hearing than most people do. This means that I can hear low-pitched sounds, as well as extremely high-pitched sounds—including the tiny squeaks of mice!

Eyes: Have you ever wondered how cats can make such accurate jumps? I have the ability to precisely judge depth, which allows me to make high jumps and prevents me from falling. My wide range of vision lets me see pretty much everywhere except behind me. I can see with less light than humans need because of my keen ability to detect motion.

Nose: My sense of smell is vital to my life. I smell everything obsessively before I eat it, which helps me decide if it is something I will be able to digest and will not make me sick. Smells also make me hungry. If my nose becomes **congested,** I might stop eating! **Respiratory** infections that lead to stuffed noses are dangerous to cats.

All Kinds of Cats

House cats might have a lot in common, but we all look a bit different. There are hundreds of different **breeds** and markings, but from the puff of a Himalayan to the flat face of a Persian, we are all just cats. Unlike dogs, which range from Chihuahua to spaniel shapes, we all are clearly very closely related.

Some Common Cat Breeds

	**Persian**	A small cat with a short, compact body and thick fur. Persians are often portrayed in paintings with royalty. They are placid and adaptable.
	**Tabby**	A cat whose fur has dark stripes on a light background. Tabbies have a distinct "M" pattern in the fur on their brows.

Some Common Cat Breeds

Bi-Color

A two-colored cat. This breed is sometimes limited to cats with a white belly, feet, and legs. Any other color can make up the rest of the body.

Siamese

An unusual-looking short-haired cat with pronounced ears and a pointed muzzle. Siamese cats have delicate bones and demanding personalities. They tend to be very vocal.

Himalayan

A cross between a fine-boned Siamese and a fluffy, interesting-looking Persian. Himalayans often have small, stocky bodies and bright blue eyes.

Ragdoll

A large, cheerful, and almost collapsible cat famous for relaxing completely in its owner's arms. Their level of **docility** is almost shockingly uncatlike.

Calico

A type of cat that has fur patched with black, white, and orange tones.

A Unique Friend

Your Furry Feline

In the wild, dogs live in packs, but cats are solitary animals, meaning that we like to live alone. You may have noticed that I keep more distance from you than other pets do. I do not want as much contact with my owner as dogs need.

However, I require attention, and humans are an important part of my life. In fact, as a kitten I develop a strong bond with the person who feeds me, grooms me, and spends time taking care of me. I can amuse myself, for instance, with a ball or by looking at birds out the window, but it delights me to hear you walk in the door. I like having you around, even if I am just napping. The relationship I have with my owner is my most important relationship, and I do not take it lightly!

Cat in the Habit

We cats are very much creatures of habit. We like to be able to predict when we will be fed, when people in our household are going to bed, and when we can expect to play or be groomed.

Looking Sharp

For the most part, I am easy to take care of. I use a litter box inside, so I do not need to go outside. My raspy tongue does a great job of removing loose hair and dirt, so I do not need to be washed. I do like to be brushed, though. Brushing helps clear my coat of extra fur, which means I will shed less and have fewer **hair balls**. Plus, getting brushed can be one of the best parts of my day. It feels really good, and it means getting attention from my owner!

As my nails grow, I **instinctively** feel the need to keep them sharp. A scratching post or board will keep me from sharpening them on furniture or walls. It is helpful to regularly clip off the sharp tips with a nail cutter.

Cat Checkup

To keep me healthy, take me to the veterinarian to get **immunized** against **rabies** and other diseases. The vet can also answer any questions about my diet or behavior. The vet will probably want to see me once every year, unless there is a reason to come back sooner.

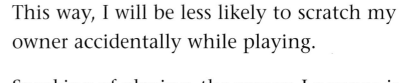

This way, I will be less likely to scratch my owner accidentally while playing.

Speaking of playing, the reason I pounce is because I'm a natural hunter. In the wild, I would catch and eat meat. Even though I am domesticated, I still need meat to be healthy. Crunchy, dry food containing high-grade meat is the best way to keep my teeth strong and my mouth clean. The amount of food I need varies with weather, activity level, and age. I also need plenty of fresh water. Milk, though delicious, is difficult for me to digest.

Purrfect!

Cats have great brains for learning tricks. While a dog likes to learn tricks to please an owner, however, I am more likely to learn them to amuse myself or to get what I want. Sometimes, though, what seems like play is my way of trying to communicate. If I knock things over one by one in the middle of the night, I may not just be playing. I may be telling you that I want attention or need to be fed. Here are some other things you might have noticed me do:

Purring: Have you ever felt my body vibrate when you pet me? The low rumble of my purring can often be felt more than heard. Mother cats purr when nursing their kittens, and kittens also purr when being fed. As an adult, I rely on purring to communicate friendly feelings when in contact with humans.

Rubbing my face: I mark my territory by rubbing my face on things or people. This leaves a scent, proving I have been in a particular place and claiming it for my own.

Grooming: I groom myself more than one quarter of the time that I am awake. I am sure you have seen me lick the inside of a paw and then rub it across my ears and face, or lean down and lick my belly or back. Grooming myself keeps me calm and happy.

The Stuff I Love

You may have also noticed me tumbling, hiding, pouncing, or attacking. Cats love to play! Some of us fetch balls and bring them to you to be thrown. Some of us like to rub our faces on **catnip** and roll in it. Others prefer to chase laser lights, small red beams that skate across the floor or up the wall. The quick movement activates our hunting instinct, and we can spend hours trying to catch the little red light.

We can also be vicious in play. You may have seen me attack a stuffed animal, grasping it with my front legs, pulling it close, and then kicking and shredding it with my back claws. I am acting on instinct.

My Favorite Things

Here are some of the things that I enjoy most:
- ▶ Sleeping about 17 hours a day.
- ▶ Lying in the sun.
- ▶ Being in high places—it's fun to look down on everyone, and it helps me feel safe.
- ▶ Stalking prey, such as a bird or mouse.
- ▶ Rolling in catnip.

This is not much different from the way a tiger in the wild might **eviscerate** a small animal. If there is nothing fun to play with—a toy or another cat—I might play rough with my owner, attacking an arm or a leg. However, it is very unlikely that I would ever seriously hurt a person.

Playing keeps me youthful, happy, and healthy. Without playing, I am more likely to become bored or depressed. If you are not eager to spend money on toys, I am just as happy to play with a ball of foil or paper, or chase a piece of ribbon or string. It is the movement of the object that catches my eye and keeps me entertained.

Cat Essentials

There are only a few things a cat like me needs to stay happy and healthy.

Collar: A collar is a place to attach tags that help identify me in case I get lost.

Bowls: I need a bowl for water and a bowl for food. It is best if each bowl is wide enough so that my whiskers will not touch the sides. This makes mealtime far more pleasurable.

Litter Box: I like a clean litter box. If you clean my litter box regularly, I will be much more likely to behave.

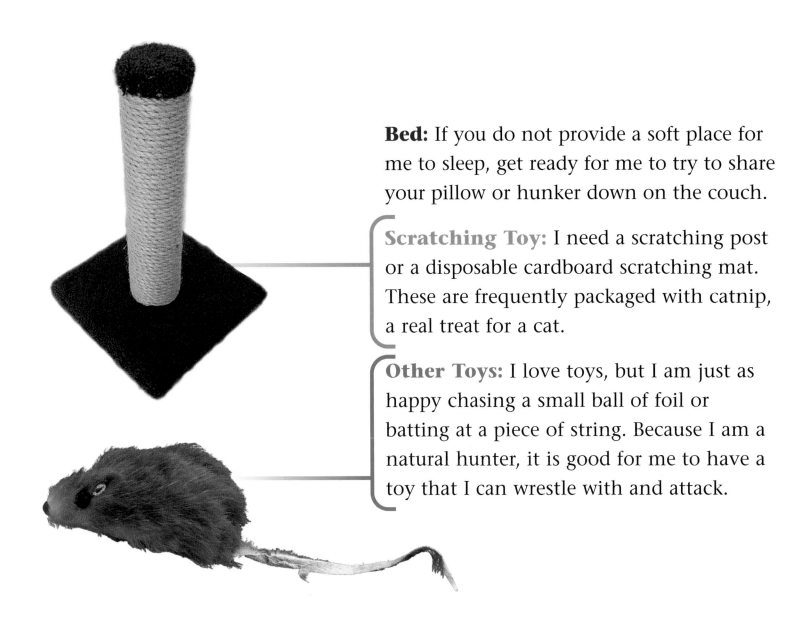

Bed: If you do not provide a soft place for me to sleep, get ready for me to try to share your pillow or hunker down on the couch.

Scratching Toy: I need a scratching post or a disposable cardboard scratching mat. These are frequently packaged with catnip, a real treat for a cat.

Other Toys: I love toys, but I am just as happy chasing a small ball of foil or batting at a piece of string. Because I am a natural hunter, it is good for me to have a toy that I can wrestle with and attack.

Planetary Meow Meow

Although cats are popular as pets, they are also often the subject of myth and focus of worship in cultures around the world.

According to the Humane Society of the United States, there are 73 million owned cats in this country, making them the nation's most popular pet.

North America

South America

In 1888, a farmer plowing in Egypt found 100,000 cat mummies!

Japan's waving cat statues depict a cat from mythology. The cat helps its owner by waving the owner out of harm's way or, in some stories, by waving away harm. In one story, a cat waves a king to shelter from bad weather. In another, a cat waves away a poisonous snake.

Asia

Europe

Africa

Australia

In India's Hindu culture, the cat is a sign of luck or plenty. Each person is responsible for feeding a cat to extend the life of his or her human family members. Many Indians also honor a cat god called Sasti.

Fun Facts Feline Focus

ZZZZMeow

One reason that kittens sleep so much is because the growth hormone is released only during sleep.

Cutting Down on Sweets

Cats cannot digest sugar, so they show little interest in eating sweets.

Flying Felines

A cat can leap about six times the length of its entire body.

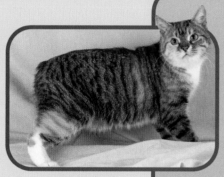

Where's the Rest of Me?

Manx cats do not have tails. This is a result of a **genetic mutation** that occurred more than 100 years ago.

Hair Per Square

Cats have about 130,000 hairs per square inch (20,155 hairs per square centimeter). That's a lot of shedding!

The Sopranos

Because cats can hear high-pitched sounds well, they tend to be more responsive to women, whose voices are higher than men's.

Record-Breakers

Can You Believe It?

HIMMY, A TABBY FROM QUEENSLAND, AUSTRALIA, has the unfortunate distinction of being the heaviest cat ever. He weighed nearly 47 pounds (21 kg).

THE OLDEST CAT ON RECORD is Puss, from Devonshire, England, who lived one day past his 36th birthday.

THE AWARD FOR TINIEST CAT EVER goes to a blue point Himalayan called Tinker Toy, who weighed 1 pound, 6 ounces (616 grams). Tinker Toy was 2.75 inches (7 cm) tall and 7.5 inches (19 cm) long.

A CAT IN TEXAS GAVE BIRTH TO 420 KITTENS over the course of her lifetime, earning her the honor of most fruitful mom.

A CAT NAMED BLACKIE was left almost 25 million dollars when his owner died!

A CAT FROM THE UNITED KINGDOM holds the record of the largest **litter** with a whopping 19 kittens.

TOWSER, A CAT IN THE EMPLOY OF SCOTLAND'S GLENTURRET DISTILLERY, reached fame when a tower was erected to commemorate her for catching nearly 30,000 mice in her lifetime.

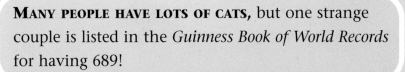

MANY PEOPLE HAVE LOTS OF CATS, but one strange couple is listed in the *Guinness Book of World Records* for having 689!

Important Dates Timeline

65M B.C. · 2000 B.C. · 400 A.D. · 1542 · 1750 · 1871 · 1919 · 1925 · 1940 · 1981 · 2000

65 million B.C. The Smilodon, a prehistoric cat with exaggerated **incisors,** is one of the most successful mammals to survive after an unknown event kills off the dinosaurs.

2000 B.C. Cats are domesticated by ancient Egyptians. Cats see the advantages—food and affection—that people can provide. In return, the Egyptians discover that their stores of grain are protected from mice and other pests. Cats enchant the culture, and Egyptians begin to worship the cat.

400–1400S A.D. Cats thrive in Europe until the Middle Ages, when they become associated with witches and viewed as agents of Satan. The widespread killing of cats helped the Black Death of the 1300s— communicated by rats— spread unchecked through Europe. This form of the bubonic plague killed one quarter of the entire European population in just four years.

1542 During the time of the Spanish Inquisition, Pope Innocent VIII condemns cats as being evil. Thousands are burned.

1750 Cats are introduced to the Americas to control pests.

1871 The first cat show is organized in London. Cat shows will later become a worldwide craze.

1919 Felix the Cat debuts as the first cartoon cat.

1925 Maurice Ravel writes an opera, *L' Enfant et les Sortileges* ("The Child and the Enchantments"), that features a song sung by cats.

1940 Tom and Jerry, the perpetually warring cat and mouse pair, star in their first theatrical cartoon, "Puss Gets the Boot."

1981 Andrew Lloyd Weber creates the musical *Cats,* based on the writer T.S. Eliot's *Old Possum's Book of Practical Cats.*

Important Cats Feline Superstars

Book Cats

Since they were first worshipped in Egypt, cats have been both a subject of devotion and a source of inspiration. Many cats have been **muses** for writers and artists. The author Colette's cats are featured in many of her stories, and Polar Bear, a white stray cat found on Christmas Eve, inspired author Cleveland Amory to write the *Cat Who Came for Christmas* series.

Hero Cats

Some cats have even helped the military. A kitty named Mourka trotted messages back and forth across a dangerous street to help Russian troops communicate during the Battle of Stalingrad. He was recognized as a hero of World War II by the *Times of London*.

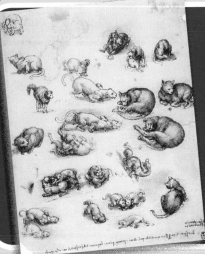

Art Cats

Cats have also inspired many artists, including Leonardo Da Vinci, who once stated, "Even the smallest feline is a work of art." Later, in the 20th century, cartoonist Jim Davis made the world fall in love with his subject, the roly-poly cat, Garfield.

Words to Know

breeds: cat classifications similar to human nationalities

catnip: a plant from the mint family with a strong smell that attracts cats

congested: having an unusual amount of mucus due to illness or infection

docility: ability to be controlled

domestic: raised or bred for human requirements

eviscerate: to remove the internal organs of an animal or human

felines: domestic cats and other members of the animal family *Felidae*

genetic mutation: a change resulting in a new biological trait or characteristic that can be passed along through different generations

hair balls: clumps of hair that accumulate in the stomach of a cat after it cleans itself

immunized: protected against disease

incisors: front teeth that are adapted to cutting

instinctively: based on strong natural impulses

litter: a group of animals born at the same time from the same mother

maneuvers: movements or actions that require skill or dexterity

muses: sources of inspiration

pedigreed: having documents recording ancestry

rabies: a virus, usually transmitted through a bite, that causes abnormal behavior and eventually death

respiratory: having to do with breathing

Where to Learn More

AT THE LIBRARY

Lachman, Larry. *Cats on the Counter.* New York: St. Martin's Press, 2002.

Shojai, Amy. *Complete Kitten Care.* New York: New American Library, 2002.

Whitely, E.H. *Understanding and Training Your Cat or Kitten.* New York: Replica Books, 2002.

ON THE WEB

For more information on cats, use FactHound to track down Web sites related to this book.

1. Go to *www.facthound.com*

2. Type in a search word related to this book or this book ID: 0756506972.

3. Click on the *Fetch It* button.

Your trusty FactHound will fetch the best Web sites for you!

ON THE ROAD

Every month throughout the year, cat shows are held all over the world. For a listing of schedules, please look at the cat show schedule pages of these associations. You will likely find a cat show near you. Awards are given in all sorts of categories.

Cat Fancier's Association
www.cfainc.org/exhibitors/show-schedule.html

American Cat Fancier's Association
www.acfacat.com/calendar.htm

American Association of Cat Enthusiasts
www.aaceinc.org/show.htm

Cat Fancier's Federation
www.cffinc.org/shows.html

INDEX

ABOUT THE AUTHOR

Meredith Phillips studied literature and Japanese language at Connecticut College and is near to completing an M.F.A. in creative nonfiction at New School University. She writes about the things she loves—animals, science, books, and food. Her writing has appeared in publications, including *The Believer*, *The Austin Chronicle*, and *The Columbia Journal*. She also works as an editorial consultant. Meredith lives in Brooklyn, New York.